# The Power of Rain

Written by Liz Miles

Collins

Rain has power.

Is the power of rain good or bad?

A bit of rain can feel good.

This hard soil is waiting for rain.

Then it rains. Seeds are hidden in the gaps.

Now look!

This herd needs rain.

The river fills up with rain. The herd gathers to lap it up.

Rain has the power to cut into rock. Hard rain fills rivers.

The rivers cut fantastic forms in the rock.

Too much rain can gush down roads.

Rain can push rocks into towns.

Rain can load rivers with mud.

Looking down, we can see the power of rain.

We need the power of rain for food.

The power of rain is good but too much rain can be bad.

# Monsoon rains

In the summer monsoons, it rains a lot.

The rain fills wells and is good for farms.

# Will it rain?

Experts can tell if it might rain.

An app can tell us how soon rain might appear.

# How much rain?

You can see how much rain you get.

See how much rain is in the pot.

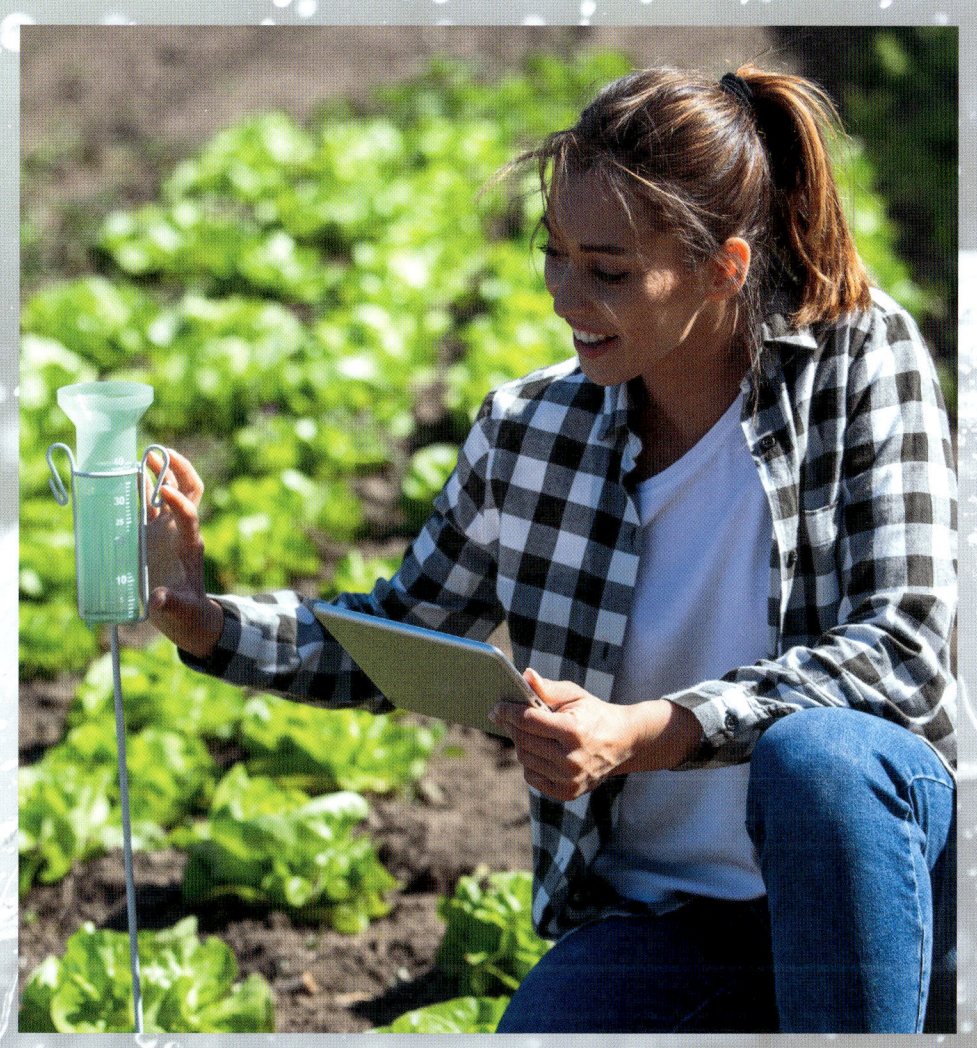

# Rain power

# Review: After reading

Use your assessment from hearing the children read to choose any GPCs, words or tricky words that need additional practice.

## Read 1: Decoding
- Ask the children to reread page 12. Encourage them to blend in their heads, silently, before reading the words aloud. Focus on **load**. Ask: What word or phrase with a similar meaning could we use instead? (e.g. *fill, pack*)
- Focus on the /er/ and /ow/ sounds. On pages 6 and 7, ask the children to identify and read the words that have an /er/ sound. (*herd, river, herd, gathers*) On page 13, ask the children to identify and read the words with the /ow/ sound. (*down, power*)
- Bonus content: Challenge the children to read pages 16 and 17. Ask them to identify the words with different /oo/ sounds. (*monsoons, good*). On page 18, point to **soon** for the children to sound out.

## Read 2: Prosody
- Turn to pages 14 and 15. Discuss how you would read these pages if you were a documentary narrator. Ask: What tone is best for the topic? (e.g. *serious*) What pace helps the listener understand? (e.g. *slow*)
- Encourage the children to read the pages aloud.
- Focus on page 15. Which words did they emphasise? (e.g. *"too much"*) Did they use a different tone for **good** and for **bad**? (e.g. *lighter tone for "good", serious tone for "bad"*)
- Bonus content: Turn to pages 16 and 17. Encourage the children to read the pages aloud in the voice of a documentary narrator.

## Read 3: Comprehension
- Ask the children to describe their experiences of rain. Ask: Was it powerful? In what way? Did it feel good or bad? Why?
- Reread pages 8 and 9. Ask: How were the fantastic forms made in the rock? Talk about the stages. Ask: What happens first? (e.g. *hard/heavy rain fills rivers*) What happens next? (e.g. *the rivers cut into the rock*)
- Use pages 22 and 23 as a prompt to talk about the power of rain. Ask: What is good about the power of rain? (e.g. *it lets plants grow and gives animals a drink*) What is bad about the power of rain? (e.g. *it can push rocks into towns and gush down roads*)